FINANCIALLY GROUNDED

Dr. Bola "Obinna" Boasmanboon
Financially Grounded

All rights reserved
Copyright © 2025 by Dr. Bola "Obinna" Boasmanboon

No part of this publication may be reproduced, distributed, or transmitted in any form or by any means, including photocopying, recording, or other electronic or mechanical methods, without the prior written permission of the publisher, except in the case of brief quotations embodied in critical reviews and certain other noncommercial uses permitted by copyright law.

Published by Spines Publishing Platform
ISBN: 979-8-90001-348-0

FINANCIALLY GROUNDED
ELIMINATE DEBT, BUILD WEALTH, AND ACHIEVE
FINANCIAL FREEDOM

DR. BOLA "OBINNA" BOASMANBOON

CONTENTS

Acknowledgments	vii
Introduction	xi
1. Understanding the Heart of Your Financial Habits	1
2. Wisdom from the Giants	7
3. The Financial Pyramid – What to Build First	13
4. The Debt Dilemma	21
5. Budgeting Is for the Bold	29
6. Savings vs. Investing–The Wealth Gap Revealed	37
7. Building Your Wealth Blueprint	45
8. Defining Financial Freedom	55
9. Protect What You Build	63
10. Wealth, Faith & Purpose	73
11. From Financial Stability to Generational Impact	81
Final Words: Your Journey Starts Now	91
Next Steps	93
Resources & Continued Support	95

ACKNOWLEDGMENTS

Writing this book has been a journey of reflection, discipline, and grace. I am deeply grateful to the many individuals who stood with me through every late night, early morning, and moment of doubt and discovery.

To my family—my beloved husband, Jerry, and our wonderful children, Jerry II, Jeremiah, and Jasmine—thank you for your constant encouragement, your prayers, and your countless sacrifices. Your unwavering support and unconditional love are the foundation upon which I continue to build.

To my friends and fellow financial professionals, thank you for challenging my thinking and sharpening my skills. Your insights and leadership have left an indelible mark on my path.

To my church family at Winners Church for All Nations, and the many communities I have had the privilege to serve, thank you for trusting me with your financial journeys. Your stories, questions, and breakthroughs are the heartbeat of this book.

To my launch team, editors, and creative partners—your excellence, faith, and feedback brought this vision to life in ways I could never have achieved alone. Thank you for believing in both the message and the messenger.

To my spiritual father, Pastor Henry Godwin (PHG), Senior Pastor of Winners Church for All Nations in Virginia, USA—thank you for your unwavering support, for not giving up on me, and for your words of encouragement when it seemed like everything was going awry. I remember during the 2024 church building project, as we were taking one of our walks and talking, you stopped, looked at me, and said, "Obinna, you have too much in you. You need to write a book." I promised that I would—and here it is, my daddy. Thank you for your prayers and, at times, your tough love. I am very grateful for your many sacrifices. Thank you for carving out valuable time from your already busy schedule to read the manuscript and provide insight and feedback. I am eternally grateful.

Above all, I give thanks to God, the true source of wisdom, strength, and provision. Without Him, this work would be impossible.

> Every good and perfect gift is from above, coming down from the Father of lights…"
>
> JAMES 1:17

May this book serve as a vessel of clarity, purpose, and hope for everyone who reads it.

With deepest appreciation,

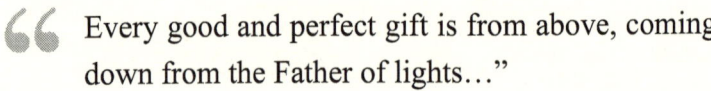

Dr. Bola "Obinna" Boasmanboon

To my husband, Jerry, and our amazing children—Jerry II, Jeremiah, and Jasmine—your love has been my anchor and your presence my motivation.

To Pastor Henry Godwin—my spiritual father, "my daddy"—thank you for believing in me when I doubted myself, for speaking life into this vision, and for standing beside me in prayer and purpose.

To God—my source, my strength, and my sustainer. Without You, this book would be empty pages. With You, it becomes purpose in print. All glory belongs to You.

To the next generation—may you never be afraid of money, but rather be equipped to master it with wisdom, grace, and Godly purpose.

To every man, woman, father, mother, and dreamer—you are not behind, you are being built.

To every person who ever felt lost in the world of money, this is for you. You do not have to be perfect to start. You only need to begin. May these words light your path, lift your spirit, and lead you home—to peace, purpose, and prosperity.

This book is for every heart seeking freedom, every mind pursuing clarity, and every soul longing to be financially grounded.

INTRODUCTION

 Money is not just about math. It is about life—about choices, fears, faith, and the future."

DR. BOLA "OBINNA" BOASMANBOON

In every family I have counseled, every boardroom I have sat in, and every classroom I have taught, one truth remains constant: financial decisions are deeply personal.

I have spent over two decades immersed in the world of finance as a student, practitioner, teacher, and coach. I earned a BBA in Accounting, an MBA in Finance and E-Business, and a Doctorate in Finance. My experience spans military service, public sector leadership, and private financial coaching. I have advised both households living paycheck to paycheck and organizations stewarding billion-dollar budgets.

One of the most defining moments of my financial career came during my very first deployment after completing Army Officer Candidate School. I was deployed in support of Operation Iraqi Freedom from December 2004 to December 2005. My primary responsibility was to reconcile the very first financial account (DSSN 8551) established in support of the war effort.

Even in times of war, financial accountability is essential. Budgeting matters. Spending within one's means is critical. And reconciliation remains non-negotiable. The officers before me had not been able to complete this task. Yet by God's grace, I— a young military officer—along with my committed team, successfully completed the reconciliation in just eight months.

During that process, we uncovered inconsistencies and pursued individuals who had attempted to defraud the federal government. At the same time, we came across accounts belonging to service members who had given their lives in the line of duty. In honor of their sacrifice, we initiated the process to relieve their outstanding debts.

That mission was not just about balancing ledgers. It was about justice, honor, and stewardship. For our work, I was awarded the Bronze Star Medal, but the recognition belongs equally to the incredible team I served with. To every fallen soldier whose records passed through our hands, your memory lives on. May you continue to rest in perfect peace.

Whether managing a military budget, a private organization's operations, a nonprofit's resources, or a household's income, one truth remains unchanged: **if the financial foundation is**

wavy and unstable, every other plan will eventually crumble. That is why I always begin with awareness, specifically, reconciliation. You must be able to account for all your money and all your money sources.

When I began working for a nonprofit organization, the very first step I took was to reconcile the books. I needed to determine what was truly on hand and where the primary sources of donations were coming from. From there, I implemented a budgetary and accountability system to manage expectations and prevent mismanagement of funds. Our books became so clean and auditable that when it was time to approach a financial institution for acquisition and renovation loans, it was not a struggle—everything was in order.

Yet, despite the difference in context, the questions remain the same:

- How do I build something that lasts?
- How do I stop living in fear or frustration?
- How do I take control of my money, instead of letting it control me?

This book was born to answer those questions—not with theory alone, but with practical wisdom, clear systems, and timeless principles.

It is for the person who feels overwhelmed by money and for the person who simply wants to do better with what they already have. It is for the ambitious and the anxious alike. It is for students, parents, pastors, entrepreneurs, and everyday people determined to live a life of meaning, not just maintenance.

WHAT MAKES THIS BOOK DIFFERENT

Many personal finance books focus exclusively on formulas or inspiration. *Financially Grounded* is designed to give you both.

- It merges timeless financial principles with today's realities
- It translates complex topics into plain, relatable language
- It centers on faith, stewardship, and values, not just accumulation
- It includes real tools, reflection prompts, and action steps you can apply immediately

You will not just read this book—you will work through it, grow with it, and return to it as your financial journey evolves.

> " The plans of the diligent lead surely to abundance, but everyone who is hasty comes only to poverty."
>
> PROVERBS 21:5

WHO THIS BOOK IS FOR

- Young professionals managing student loans and career transitions
- Couples trying to align their financial goals and avoid money conflicts
- Faith-based individuals seeking biblical and practical financial guidance
- Entrepreneurs balancing business and personal wealth goals
- Anyone ready to move from confusion to clarity and from stress to strategy

Whether you are recovering from a financial setback, building from scratch, or seeking to scale your success, this book offers a grounded, values-based roadmap forward.

WHAT YOU CAN EXPECT

Each chapter blends:

- Storytelling–to humanize the numbers
- Principles–drawn from timeless wisdom and real-world experience
- Practical tools–such as templates, frameworks, and next steps
- Reflection prompts–to help you align your money with your values

This is not about quick fixes. It is about transformation—the kind that starts with a mindset shift and ends with a generational impact.

LET US BEGIN

You may be here because you are tired of struggling, unsure about the next step, or you are ready to finally get your financial house in order. No matter your starting point, the good news is this:

> It is not too late. You are not too far behind. And you do not have to figure it out alone."
>
> DR. BOLA "OBINNA" BOASMANBOON

Together, we will build a financial life that is not only successful but significant.

Let us begin a journey that is financially strong, spiritually sound, and eternally grounded.

CHAPTER 1
UNDERSTANDING THE HEART OF YOUR FINANCIAL HABITS

Money decisions are rarely just about dollars and cents. They are about stories—about identity, fear, pride, and faith. Before we break down budgets, investments, or wealth strategies, we must first confront the person behind the wallet. Who you are, how you were raised, and what you believe about money are all shaping your financial decisions—whether you realize it or not.

In my years of studying and teaching finance, I have seen a consistent truth: lasting wealth does not begin with math; it begins with meaning. People do not change financially because they found a better spreadsheet. They change because they discovered a better reason.

MONEY MEMORIES: WHAT SHAPED YOU?

We all have financial memories—some empowering, others painful. Think back to your childhood.

- Was money a source of stress or celebration?
- Was it talked about openly or avoided like a bad word?
- Did you learn to view money as a tool, a burden, a reward—or something else?

I grew up in a small village in Nigeria, where financial struggle was very real. I was raised by my maternal grandmother, a resilient woman who stretched her limited resources not only to care for me and my cousins living with her but also to help other children in the community. We did not have much. I remember sleeping on woven mats because there were not enough mattresses, being sent home from school for not having writing materials and wearing school uniforms with patches because we could not afford new ones.

I have also watched how the presence or absence of money could influence a family's emotions, decisions, and even their relationships. That early exposure stayed with me. It made me curious. It pushed me to learn, and it ultimately shaped my purpose: to help others take control of their financial story.

These early scripts matter more than we think. Most people do not just manage money; they repeat what they saw. Financial healing starts when we pause long enough to ask: What belief am I living out, and is it serving me well?

YOUR MONEY PERSONALITY

Financial behavior is not random. It is driven by personality, experience, and emotional patterns. You might recognize yourself in one of these categories:

- **The Spender**: Generous and expressive but often impulsive
- **The Saver**: Disciplined and secure, but sometimes hesitant to enjoy
- **The Avoider**: Overwhelmed by money and prefers not to deal with it
- **The Planner**: Organized and strategic, thrives on control and systems

No identity is better or worse, but self-awareness gives you power. When you know how you are wired, you can start designing financial decisions that support your goals instead of sabotaging them.

FROM SCARCITY TO STEWARDSHIP

Many people live in a state of financial fear—always bracing for the next emergency, always feeling like there is never quite enough. However, there is a better way to live.

Stewardship shifts the mindset from survival to strategy. It says: I have been entrusted with something valuable. I have a responsibility to manage it with purpose.

I have learned this principle in both my faith and finance work: financial peace does not come from having more but from managing what you already have with diligence. One timeless principle I often teach is this: Start by keeping a portion of what you earn—no matter how small—and let that be the seed of your future wealth.

That simple habit, practiced with discipline, has changed more financial futures than any investment tip I could offer.

> Wisdom is the principal thing; therefore get wisdom: and with all thy getting get understanding."

PROVERBS 4:7

ACADEMIC LENS: WHY BEHAVIORAL FINANCE MATTERS

Behavioral finance—a field that explores how psychology affects financial decisions—reveals something profound: people are rarely rational with money.

Common behavioral patterns include:

- **Loss Aversion**: We fear losing $100 more than we enjoy gaining $100
- **Confirmation Bias**: We tend to see only the data that agrees with what we already believe

- **Present Bias:** We prioritize today's pleasure over tomorrow's gain

As a finance professional and educator, I have studied these concepts in theory. However, in practice, they play out in everyday decisions—from swiping a credit card impulsively to putting off retirement savings.

Financial mastery does not start with willpower—it starts with awareness.

THE POWER OF YOUR WHY

You do not need another budget or investment strategy until you reconnect with your why. Why do you want financial change?

- To stop living paycheck to paycheck?
- To travel, start a business, or give generously?
- To break generational cycles and model something different for your children?

Your why is what gets you through when your motivation fades. It anchors you when the process feels slow. Without it, even the best financial plan will fall apart.

One principle I teach my clients early is simple but powerful: Money flows best when it has a mission. Wealth does not come from hustle alone—it comes from alignment.

REFLECTION QUESTIONS

1. What is your earliest memory of money?
2. What did your parents or caregivers teach you (directly or indirectly) about money?
3. How do you currently feel when managing your finances—confident, anxious, guilty, indifferent?
4. What is your personal "why" for building wealth?

KEY TAKEAWAYS

- Financial behavior is rooted in memory, identity, and belief.
- Knowing your money personality helps guide better choices.
- Stewardship shifts your focus from lack to responsibility.
- Behavioral finance teaches us that awareness precedes change.
- A strong "why" anchors your financial journey and drives real progress.

Next up: We will explore time-tested wisdom from some of the most impactful voices in finance—and learn how to apply their principles with modern-day clarity and personal conviction.

CHAPTER 2
WISDOM FROM THE GIANTS

LEARNING FROM THE VOICES WHO CHANGED THE MONEY CONVERSATION

When you are serious about building wealth, the first step is not inventing something new—it is learning from those who have done it well. Over the years, I have drawn from a wide range of voices in personal finance, both modern and timeless. Some of these have become household names. Others have been quietly shaping minds for generations.

However, no matter their background or approach, they all agree on a few universal truths: spend less than you earn, protect what you have, and be intentional with every dollar. These are not just financial strategies—they are life principles.

In this chapter, we will explore some of the most influential minds in the personal finance space, not to idolize them but to extract what works and leave what does not.

DAVE RAMSEY: DISCIPLINE AND DIRECTION

Dave Ramsey's impact on American households is undeniable. He offers a clear, straightforward path out of debt and into financial stability. His "baby steps" have helped millions develop the habit of discipline—something that cannot be bought but can build a future.

Where Ramsey is most effective is in showing people how to take control. He turns overwhelm into momentum, guiding people from chaos to clarity with simple, actionable steps.

What I have learned in my own work is that structure creates peace. It is not about rigid rules but about making decisions with confidence. Whether you are using cash envelopes or apps, the power is in consistency.

At the core, his philosophy aligns with an ancient truth: if you desire to build wealth, first learn to master yourself. That principle has never gone out of style.

SUZE ORMAN: COURAGE AND PROTECTION

Suze Orman shifted the conversation from just "How much do you have?" to "What does your money say about your self-worth?" She is passionate about making sure people are protected, emotionally and financially.

From estate planning to insurance to the psychological weight of financial decisions, she brings attention to the person behind the plan. In many ways, she reminds us that building wealth is not just about knowledge—it is about courage.

In my own experience coaching others, I have seen that many people are not stuck because of numbers; they are stuck because of fear. The moment you believe you are worthy of protection, investment, and freedom, you begin to act differently.

And when it comes to financial storms—whether emotional or economic—it is not about if they will come, but when. Preparation is the most loving thing you can do for your future self and your family.

DR. OLUMIDE EMMANUEL: FAITH AND FINANCIAL PURPOSE

Dr. Emmanuel brings a global and spiritual perspective that is refreshing and necessary. His work is centered on the idea that wealth has a mission and that money is a servant, not a master.

What resonates most with me is his emphasis on responsibility. Whether you are managing $100 or $1,000,000, the question is the same: Are you being faithful with what you have been given?

This mindset of stewardship echoes across faith traditions and financial disciplines. It is not just about building wealth—it is about being trusted with it. That trust starts with how you handle today's decisions, not tomorrow's windfall.

TIMELESS PRINCIPLES IN ACTION

Long before modern financial gurus hit the airwaves, universal truths were being practiced by those who built and preserved wealth. One of the simplest and most powerful is this: Always keep a portion of what you earn.

This principle—to live on less than you make—is echoed in every enduring financial philosophy. Call it tithing, paying yourself first, or wealth preservation—the message is the same: **You must learn to hold on to what you receive before you can multiply it.**

Another principle is to put every dollar to work. Money that sits idle is at risk of erosion. However, money that is invested wisely—whether through business, savings, or training—begins to grow. This is not just good math; it is good stewardship.

And finally, protect your money from unnecessary loss. Be cautious with where you place your trust, read the fine print, and never invest in what you do not understand. These are not just habits of the wealthy—they are habits that make people wealthy.

BRINGING IT ALL TOGETHER: A BALANCED MODEL

What I appreciate most about these financial voices—and the ancient principles that still apply—is that each fills a different gap:

- Ramsey offers structure and momentum.

- Orman brings protection and empowerment.
- Emmanuel instills purpose and values.
- Timeless wisdom offers simplicity, clarity, and direction.

The key is not to follow one voice blindly but to find an alignment between proven principles and your personal values. The best financial plan is one that honors your life, your culture, and your convictions.

You do not need a celebrity guru. You need a model that makes sense for where you are and where you are going.

REFLECTION QUESTIONS

1. Which financial voice or philosophy do you connect with the most right now, and why?
2. Do you need more structure, more emotional clarity, or more spiritual alignment in your financial life?
3. What is one timeless principle you have ignored in the past that you are now ready to apply?
4. Are you building a financial strategy that truly reflects your values and purpose?

KEY TAKEAWAYS

- Every financial expert brings a valuable piece of the puzzle—the goal is integration, not imitation.

- True wealth-building requires discipline, courage, and stewardship.
- Timeless principles like saving first, investing wisely, and protecting your money never go out of style.
- The most powerful financial model is one that reflects your purpose, not just your paycheck.

Next up: We will lay your financial foundation—starting with the essentials of budgeting, emergency planning, and the step-by-step pyramid that keeps your financial house standing strong.

CHAPTER 3
THE FINANCIAL PYRAMID – WHAT TO BUILD FIRST

LAYING A STRONG FINANCIAL FOUNDATION BEFORE REACHING FOR WEALTH

You would not build a house starting with the roof—yet that is exactly what many people do with money. They want to invest, start businesses, or buy property, but they have skipped the foundational steps. As a result, their financial structures collapse when life gets unpredictable.

This is why I teach the Financial Pyramid—a framework that builds wealth from the ground up. It ensures that your financial life is protected, stable, and scalable. Whether you are starting from scratch or rebuilding after a setback, these levels create a lasting blueprint.

WHY A PYRAMID?

The pyramid is a timeless symbol of strength, order, and intentional growth. Its wide base offers stability. Its shape demands discipline. Financially speaking, it means this: **you must secure the essentials before reaching for expansion.**

This approach mirrors a powerful truth I often share with clients —that wealth is not built overnight but over time by stacking one wise decision atop another. The ancient principle of "first, fatten thy purse" echoes here: before you grow wealth, you must protect it, and before you protect it, you must understand it.

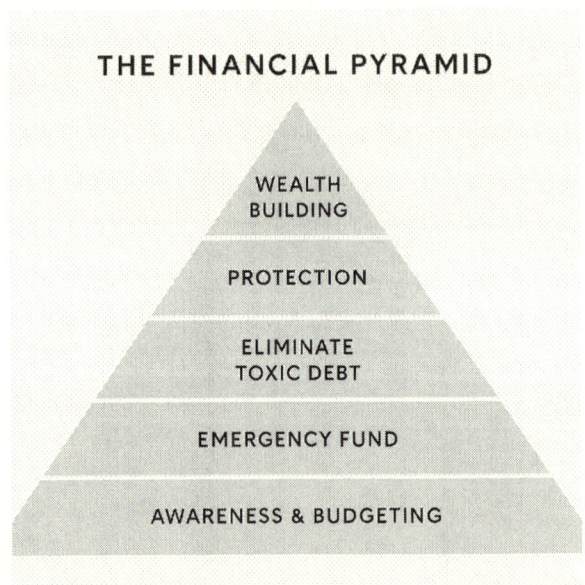

LEVEL 1: FINANCIAL AWARENESS & BUDGETING

You cannot master what you do not measure. That is why the base of the pyramid is awareness—knowing what comes in, what goes out, and where your money is actually going.

Key Actions:

- Track all sources of income.
- List every expense—fixed, variable, and hidden.
- Choose a budgeting method (zero-based, 50/30/20, envelope system, or app-based).

Why It Matters:

Budgeting is not punishment. It is permission—permission to spend with purpose, to prioritize what matters, and to sleep at night knowing your bills are paid. A clear budget helps you stop guessing and start deciding.

When you assign every dollar a role, you are not limiting your money—you are leading it.

LEVEL 2: EMERGENCY FUND – YOUR FINANCIAL CUSHION

Before investing or paying off major debt, build your cushion. Life will throw surprises—illness, layoffs, home repairs. An emergency fund helps you meet them without panic.

Key Actions:

- Save $1,000 as a starter fund.
- Build to 3–6 months of essential expenses.

Why It Matters:

An emergency fund prevents crises from turning into catastrophes. It also guards your progress, so you do not have to dip into retirement savings or rack up credit card debt when the unexpected happens.

This is what it means to "guard thy treasures from loss." Without protection, even the wisest plan can fall apart.

LEVEL 3: ELIMINATE TOXIC DEBT

Debt is not all evil, but some of it is dangerous. High-interest consumer debt—especially credit cards and payday loans—will strangle your financial growth.

Key Actions:

- List all debts by balance and interest rate.
- Choose a payoff method: Debt Snowball (smallest balance first) or Debt Avalanche (highest interest first).
- Avoid new debt while paying off the old.

Why It Matters:

You cannot build true wealth if your income is constantly going to lenders. Paying off toxic debt gives you your income—and your future—back.

Debt is not just a financial issue. It is emotional and spiritual, too. It can make you feel stuck, ashamed, or small. Getting out of debt is not just about numbers—it is about freedom.

LEVEL 4: PROTECTION – INSURANCE AND LEGAL BASICS

Once your money is flowing and your debt is shrinking, you must protect what you are building. Just like a fortress needs a wall, your finances need defense mechanisms.

Key Actions:

- Ensure proper health, life, auto, and disability insurance.
- Have a will, power of attorney, and healthcare directive in place.
- If applicable, review estate planning options like a trust.

Why It Matters:

A single lawsuit, illness, or accident can wipe out decades of progress. Insurance and legal documents are not for the wealthy—they are for the wise.

Wealth is not only what you accumulate—it is what you preserve.

LEVEL 5: LONG-TERM WEALTH PLANNING

With your foundation set, now you can begin building. This is where you shift from stability to growth, letting your money work harder than you do.

Key Components:

- Retirement accounts (401(k), Roth IRA, SEP IRA, Thrift Savings).
- Investment accounts (index funds, ETFs, mutual funds).
- Real estate, intellectual property, or business ventures.

Why It Matters:

At this level, compound interest becomes your partner. Consistency matters more than complexity. And discipline outweighs hype. You do not need to chase trends. You need to follow time-tested truths—start early, stay steady, and let your wealth grow like a tree planted by water.

As one timeless financial principle puts it: "Gold grows when it is wisely invested. It flees when left idle or spent unwisely." Long-term planning is the difference between busy money and building money.

FINANCIAL PYRAMID SUMMARY

Here is a simple recap of the pyramid structure:

1. **Awareness & Budgeting** –Know your numbers.
2. **Emergency Fund** – Protect against the unexpected.
3. **Eliminate Toxic Debt** – Stop financial bleeding.
4. **Protection** – Guard what you have built
5. **Wealth Building** – Invest and multiply.

Trying to build wealth without this order is like planting seeds on rocky soil. You may see growth, but it will not last.

REFLECTION QUESTIONS

1. Which level of the pyramid are you currently working on?
2. Have you ever tried to skip steps, and what were the consequences?
3. What is one action you can take this week to strengthen your foundation?
4. What habit or mindset shift would help you stay consistent at your current level?

KEY TAKEAWAYS

- Financial growth must be built in order: awareness first, then protection, then growth.

- The Financial Pyramid creates a strong foundation for lasting wealth.
- Small steps, taken in the right order, lead to big outcomes over time.
- Success is not in skipping ahead—it is in mastering each layer fully and faithfully.

Next up: We will dig deeper into debt—how to tell the difference between strategic and toxic borrowing and how to break free from the emotional and financial weight of debt for good.

CHAPTER 4
THE DEBT DILEMMA

BREAKING FREE OR BUILDING SMART: WHAT YOU REALLY NEED TO KNOW ABOUT DEBT

Debt is one of the most emotionally loaded topics in personal finance. Some see it as a tool. Others see it as a trap. And for many, it is both, depending on how and why it is used.

The reality is simple: debt decisions can either accelerate your progress or anchor your potential. In this chapter, we will sort through the different kinds of debt, examine the mindsets that surround them, and explore strategies to either escape debt or leverage it wisely.

THE EMOTIONAL WEIGHT OF DEBT

Debt is not just financial—it is psychological. It whispers in the back of your mind when you are trying to sleep. It causes friction in relationships. It feeds guilt and fear, even when your income is steady.

- You can feel like you are drowning even if you earn six figures.
- You can carry shame even if you are making your payments on time.
- You can delay dreams—starting a family, launching a business, buying a home—all because of debt.

Here is what you need to hear: Debt does not define you. You are not broken. And there is a way forward—no matter where you are starting.

FINANCIAL STRUGGLES AND MARITAL STRAIN

Finances are a major stressor in relationships and a significant contributing factor in divorce:

- 20–40% of divorces are attributed in part to financial problems.
- 22% of divorces are caused primarily by money issues, making it the third most common cause behind incompatibility and infidelity.
- Nearly one-third of couples cite cost-of-living stress as a reason for marital breakdown or divorce.
- About 10% of those who experienced financial infidelity reported it led directly to divorce.

- Among couples who divorced due to finances, 38% took on $10,000+ in additional debt, and 40% saw credit scores drop over 50 points.

These numbers reveal a sobering truth: financial instability and broken trust around money are not just financial issues—they become emotional and spiritual wounds in relationships.

UNDERSTANDING THE TYPES OF DEBT

Not all debt is created equal. Some debt steals. Other debt can serve. However, all debt must be understood and managed, not ignored.

Type of Debt	Category	Example Use	Considerations
Credit Card Debt	Toxic	Consumer purchases	High interest, avoid or pay off monthly
Student Loans	Conditional	Higher education	Acceptable if ROI (return on investment) is high
Mortgage	Productive	Homeownership	Consider fixed rates, equity potential
Business Loans	Strategic	Capital for expansion	Only when backed by solid business model
Auto Loans	Depreciating	Transportation	Only if interest is low and car is reliable

Dr. Emmanuel brings a biblical and African cultural lens to the conversation. His principle is simple:

 The borrower is slave to the lender."

PROVERBS 22:7

Ask yourself this: Will this debt increase my income or long-term net worth?

If the answer is no, proceed with caution. If the answer is yes, you still need a plan to manage it wisely.

THE INVISIBLE COST: MENTAL AND FINANCIAL FREEDOM

There is a hidden cost to every debt—and it is not just interest. It is stress. It is indecision. It is the weight of owing someone else before you have even begun the month.

Ancient wisdom teaches that borrowing should be approached with humility and strategy. To borrow without a plan is to invite servitude. And in truth, many people have traded their futures for fleeting pleasures—not because they lacked intelligence, but because they lacked perspective.

Whether you call it "modern convenience" or "financial slavery," the result is the same: debt creates limitations. Freedom comes from ownership.

BREAKING FREE: TWO PROVEN PAYOFF STRATEGIES

There is no one-size-fits-all when it comes to debt elimination. However, there are two widely used and effective strategies:

1. **Debt Snowball**

- Pay off your smallest debt first
- Roll that payment into the next smallest, and so on
- Builds quick momentum and emotional wins

Best for: People who need visible progress to stay motivated

2. **Debt Avalanche: Pay off the highest-interest debt first to reduce overall cost.**

- Pay off the highest-interest debt first
- Focus on mathematical savings over emotion
- Reduces total interest paid

Best for: Those motivated by logic and long-term payoff

Both methods work—if you stay consistent. Some people even combine them: start with a small win to build motivation, then shift to highest-interest accounts for long-term gains.

WHAT ABOUT CREDIT SCORES?

Credit scores can feel like a measuring stick for financial worth —but they are not. **A credit score simply tracks how well you manage debt**, not how much wealth you have.

While your score may dip temporarily as you pay off accounts or stop using credit, that is a short-term shift. Your focus should be on net worth, not creditworthiness. Do not stay in debt just to maintain a number that does not build your future.

STRATEGIC DEBT: WHEN BORROWING CAN MAKE SENSE

Though debt should never be entered into lightly, there are cases where it can be a tool—when backed by purpose and a clear return on investment.

Strategic borrowing could include:

- A mortgage that builds equity and reduces your housing cost over time
- A business loan tied to a proven income stream or contract
- Education funding that leads directly to a career with long-term growth

Even then, the rule remains: borrow only what you can repay comfortably and always protect your margin.

As one timeless principle teaches: Only borrow what you could repay if the wind stopped blowing and the waters stopped flowing.

FREEDOM OVER FLATTERY: SAYING NO TO PRESSURE

In a world where debt is normalized—"no payments for 6 months," "zero down today," "instant approval"—choosing to live within your means is countercultural.

However, those who choose freedom over flattery build peace. It is not about impressing others. It is about honoring yourself and your future.

YOUR PRACTICAL DEBT ELIMINATION PLAN

1. List all your debts—balances, interest rates, and minimum payments.
2. Choose your payoff method—snowball, avalanche, or hybrid.
3. Find extra cash flow—cut expenses, boost income, redirect windfalls.
4. Automate payments—consistency wins over time
5. Track and celebrate progress—motivation matters.
6. Avoid new debt—do not reopen wounds while healing.

REFLECTION QUESTIONS

1. What kind of debt do you currently carry, and how does it make you feel emotionally and spiritually?
2. Have financial tensions ever caused conflict or distance in your relationships?

3. Are you more motivated by short-term wins or long-term savings?
4. How might resolving financial stress strengthen your marriage and future legacy?

KEY TAKEAWAYS

- Debt can either fuel growth or fuel bondage—know which you are dealing with.
- Not all debt is toxic, but all debt requires a plan.
- Emotional freedom is as important as financial savings.
- Payoff strategies work best when paired with consistent action.
- The goal is not just to be debt-free—it is to be free, period.

Next up: We will dive into one of the most misunderstood and undervalued practices in personal finance—budgeting. Get ready to rethink everything you thought budgeting was and discover how it can empower you to lead your money instead of being led by it.

CHAPTER 5
BUDGETING IS FOR THE BOLD

RECLAIMING CONTROL OVER EVERY DOLLAR YOU EARN

 Suppose one of you wants to build a tower. Won't you first sit down and estimate the cost to see if you have enough money to complete it?"

LUKE 14:28 (NIV)

If the word "budget" makes you cringe, you are not alone. To many, budgeting feels like punishment—restrictive, boring, and a constant reminder of what you cannot have. However, that view is outdated and misleading.

A budget is not a prison. It is a plan. It is not about saying "no" to life—it is about saying "yes" to what matters most.

Creating a budget takes courage. It requires you to be honest, focused, and proactive. It is one of the boldest things you can do with your money.

THE BUDGETING MYTH: IT IS NOT JUST FOR THE BROKE

One of the most dangerous financial assumptions is that budgeting is only for people who are struggling. The truth is, the more money you earn, the more essential a budget becomes.

Without a plan, money has a way of slipping through your fingers. I have worked with high-income earners who did not know where their money went—and have heard of school teachers who built six-figure net worths on a clear, consistent plan.

Budgeting is not about how much you make—it is about how much you keep, how much you use wisely, and how much you grow.

A budget is:

- A plan for your money before the month begins.
- A mirror that reflects your real priorities.
- A tool that eliminates waste and creates margin.
- A guide that keeps your emotions from hijacking your goals.

When you assign every dollar a job, you are taking authority.

You are saying: "This money works for me, not the other way around."

> THE WISDOM HERE IS SIMPLE:
> MONEY LEFT WITHOUT PURPOSE WILL ALWAYS FIND SOMETHING UNPRODUCTIVE TO DO.

CHOOSING YOUR BUDGETING METHOD

There is no perfect method. The best budget is the one you will actually stick to. Here are four popular options to consider:

1. Zero-Based Budgeting
Every dollar gets assigned a job—income minus expenses equals zero.
Best for: People who like precision and control.
Tools: EveryDollar, YNAB, Excel.

2. 50/30/20 Rule
Divide your income: 50% needs, 30% wants, 20% savings/debt repayment.
Best for: Simplicity and quick setup.
Tools: Mint, Goodbudget.

3. Envelope System
Use cash (or digital envelopes) for each spending category.
Best for: Those who overspend with cards.
Modern options: Qube Money, Mvelopes.

4. Hybrid Budget

Mix tech, spreadsheets, and automation for a custom setup.

Best for: Tech-savvy users who like flexibility and tracking.

CREATING (OR RESETTING) YOUR BUDGET

Start simple. Here is how:

1. Know Your Income Use net income — what actually hits your account. Include side gigs, support payments, etc.

2. Give Your First Fruits As Christians, we honor God by giving our tithe—10% of our income—before addressing any other expenses. This first fruit offering acknowledges God's provision and his rightful place in our finances. Scripture teaches us this principle throughout the Bible. Malachi 3:10 reminds us that when we bring our whole tithe into the storehouse, God promises to open the floodgates of heaven and pour out blessings we don't have room to store. This reflects the biblical truth that faithfulness in giving honors God and invites his blessing into our lives.

3. List Your Expenses Start with essentials: housing, groceries, transportation, insurance. Then, add variable spending: subscriptions, dining out, and entertainment.

4. Assign Every Dollar Use your chosen method to give every remaining dollar a job after your tithe. Make room for saving, giving beyond the tithe, and debt reduction.

5. Track Weekly Budgets are not static. Review regularly to stay on track.

6. Adjust Monthly Life changes — your budget should, too. Update it based on new goals, income shifts, or spending trends.

BOLD BUDGETING = VALUE-BASED LIVING

The most powerful budgets are not built on guilt—they are built on values. Your spending should reflect your priorities, not your impulses.

If generosity matters to you, make space for it.

If freedom is your goal, protect your savings.

If travel brings you joy, plan for it without shame.

Budgeting is about alignment. It is your personal declaration: "I refuse to drift. I choose to direct."

WHY MOST BUDGETS FAIL

- They are too rigid.
- They ignore real habits.
- They do not account for emotional spending.
- The budgeter never tracks or adjusts.

The solution? Build flexibility. Budget for joy and responsibility. And check in regularly—your budget is not "set and forget," it is "plan and adapt."

SCHOLAR'S LENS: PSYCHOLOGY AND BUDGET SUCCESS

As someone who has studied finance academically and coached real people through their financial journeys, I have seen this truth again and again: Most budget failures are not about math—they are about mindset.

We spend out of emotion, habit, or fatigue. Stress, boredom, and social influence all impact spending more than logic does.

Pro tip: Sync your budget with your calendar. Anticipate high-spending days (weekends, holidays, emotionally vulnerable periods) and plan accordingly.

This is how you move from reactive to intentional.

REFLECTION QUESTIONS

1. What is your current budgeting method (if any), and does it work for you?
2. How does the idea of budgeting make you feel—restricted, empowered, overwhelmed?
3. What are your top three financial priorities right now? Does your spending reflect them?
4. Are you ready to start, restart, or upgrade your budgeting system?

KEY TAKEAWAYS

- Budgeting is an act of empowerment, not punishment.
- Your budget should reflect your values, not just your bills.
- Flexibility, honesty, and consistency are more important than perfection.
- Bold budgeting brings peace, purpose, and control.

Next up: We will tackle the difference between saving and investing—when to do each, why both matter and how to make your money multiply without sacrificing your peace of mind.

CHAPTER 6
SAVINGS VS. INVESTING—THE WEALTH GAP REVEALED

HOW TO GROW YOUR MONEY WITHOUT LOSING YOUR MIND

Most people are taught how to save money. Fewer are taught how to grow it.

You may have been told to "save for a rainy day," but no one explained how inflation slowly erodes the value of your savings. Perhaps you have heard about the stock market but avoided it because you were afraid of losing everything.

Here is the truth: Saving is essential, but saving alone will not build wealth.

To break out of financial survival mode and enter the realm of financial freedom, you must understand both saving and investing—and how to use each wisely.

THE PURPOSE OF SAVING

Saving is about short-term security. It provides peace of mind. It prepares you for the unexpected. It sets the stage for bigger moves.

WHEN YOU SHOULD SAVE:

- To build or maintain your emergency fund.
- For short-term goals (e.g., a vacation, down payment, or wedding).
- When you anticipate a large upcoming expense.
- As a buffer between paychecks if your income is variable.

BEST TOOLS FOR SAVING:

- High-yield savings accounts (HYSAs).
- Money market accounts.
- Certificates of deposit (CDs).
- Traditional savings accounts (as a last resort).

Limitations:

- Low interest rates mean your money will not grow significantly.
- Inflation reduces purchasing power over time.
- Saving is safe, but it does not multiply wealth.

Key Message: Saving is about preservation. Investing is about multiplication.

 The wise store up choice food and olive oil, but fools gulp theirs down."

PROVERBS 21:20

THE POWER OF INVESTING

Investing is about long-term growth. It is how you make your money work for you.

Done wisely, investing builds wealth passively, with time and consistency doing most of the heavy lifting.

WHY INVEST:

- To outpace inflation.
- To build wealth for retirement, legacy, and financial freedom.
- To diversify your income and reduce reliance on your paycheck.
- To take advantage of compound interest—growth on your growth.

COMMON INVESTMENT VEHICLES

Type	Description	Risk Level	Goal
Stocks	Ownership in a company	Medium to high	Growth
Bonds	Lending money to a government/corporation	Low to medium	Stability/income
Mutual Funds	Professionally managed bundles of assets	Medium	Diversified growth
ETFs	Funds traded like stocks, often lower cost	Medium	Low-cost diversification
Real Estate	Income from rental or appreciation	Medium to high	Cash flow and value
Retirement Accounts	Tax-advantaged investment tools	Varies	Long-term wealth building

THE WEALTH GAP: WHAT HAPPENS IF YOU DO NOT INVEST

Consider this example:

Monique (Saver): Saves $500 per month in a savings account, earning 1%.

Marcus (Investor): Invests $500 per month in a fund averaging 8%.

Timeframe: 30 years.

Name	Monthly Contribution	Total Contribution	End Balance
Monique	$500	$180,000	~$208,000
Marcus	$500	$180,000	~$745,000

Difference: Over $500,000—with the same contribution.

That is the wealth gap. Saving helps you hold your place. Investing moves you forward.

COMMON FEARS ABOUT INVESTING (AND THE TRUTH)

1. **"I do not know enough."** Start simple with index funds or retirement accounts. Learn as you go.
2. **"What if I lose everything?"** Diversification and time help reduce risk. Volatility is normal. Growth is historical.
3. **"Is investing gambling?"** No. Investing is a calculated, informed strategy. Gambling is pure chance.
4. **"I do not have enough money to invest."** Many platforms let you start with as little as $5 to $50. Start where you are.

Goal	Use Saving	Use Investing
Emergency Fund	✓	✗
Vacation in 6 months	✓	✗
Retirement in 30 years	✗	✓
Home purchase in 3–5 years	✓ (or CDs)	Maybe (low risk)
Building generational wealth	✗	✓

Think of it this way: Save for safety. Invest for legacy.

FAITH, WISDOM, AND MULTIPLICATION

Wealth is not created through hoarding—it is created through multiplying what you have been given. Investing wisely is an act of stewardship. It allows your resources to grow and serve greater purposes—whether that means blessing your family, supporting your community, or funding your mission.

Investing is not just about gaining more. It is about becoming more—more capable, more generous, more grounded.

 Invest in seven ventures, yes, in eight; you do not know what disaster may come upon the land."

ECCLESIASTES 11:2

SCHOLAR'S LENS: UNDERSTANDING RISK AND TIME

In financial theory, one of the most critical principles is your **time horizon**:

- The longer you can leave money invested, the more risk you can afford to take.
- The more risk you can manage, the greater your potential return.

OTHER KEY CONCEPTS:

- **Diversification** reduces your risk by spreading it.
- **Dollar-Cost Averaging** smooths market ups and downs over time.
- **Compound Interest** builds wealth exponentially—it is interest on your interest.

From both an academic and practical standpoint, you do not need to beat the market. You simply need to be in the market—consistently and patiently.

REFLECTION QUESTIONS

1. Are you currently more of a saver, an investor, or neither?
2. What fears or beliefs are holding you back from investing?
3. What is one financial goal that could be accelerated by smart investing?
4. Have you reviewed your savings and investment allocation recently?

KEY TAKEAWAYS

- Saving and investing serve different purposes—both are essential.
- Saving preserves. Investing multiplies.

- Inflation makes saving alone insufficient for wealth-building
- Time and consistency are more powerful than market timing.
- Investing is not gambling—it is strategic, disciplined stewardship.

Next up: We will design your personal Wealth Blueprint—a step-by-step guide to building multiple income streams, strengthening your assets, and creating a life of financial independence.

CHAPTER 7
BUILDING YOUR WEALTH BLUEPRINT

DESIGNING A LIFE WITH INCOME, IMPACT, AND INDEPENDENCE

Up to this point, you have laid your foundation: you have developed awareness, built a safety cushion, tackled debt, created a working budget, and begun to understand the difference between saving and investing. Now, it is time to shift from financial stability to financial strategy.

Wealth is not just about how much you earn—it's about how you **build, manage, and multiply** your resources over time. This chapter is about intentional wealth creation—not through guesswork or gimmicks, but through a clear, personalized plan. A Wealth Blueprint is not a one-time document. It is a living system that aligns your income streams, asset growth, spending, and values.

The plans of the diligent lead surely to abundance, but everyone who is hasty comes only to poverty."

PROVERBS 21:5

WHAT IS A WEALTH BLUEPRINT?

A wealth blueprint is a step-by-step plan for building financial independence using a combination of the following:

- **Active income**—earned from employment or self-employment.
- **Passive income**—generated from investments, rental properties, or intellectual property.
- **Asset growth**—appreciation in real estate, retirement funds, and business equity.
- **Cash flow management**—how well you control what comes in and what goes out.

This is your personal financial GPS. It does not guarantee easy success, but it does give you direction, clarity, and confidence.

Think of it as a business plan for your personal finances—rooted in your goals, values, and long-term vision.

Without a blueprint, we don't build. We drift.

STEP 1: UNDERSTAND AND EXPAND YOUR INCOME STREAMS

Most people rely on a single income stream—usually their job. This puts them in a vulnerable position. Wealthy individuals tend to diversify, creating multiple income streams that reduce risk and increase opportunity.

Categories of Income:

- Earned Income: Wages or salary from a job.
- Business Income: Profits from a business or side hustle.
- Interest Income: Earnings from savings, lending, or bonds.
- Dividend Income: Payouts from stock investments.
- Rental Income: From real estate properties.
- Capital Gains: Profit from selling assets.
- Residual/Royalty Income: Earnings from books, courses, licenses, or patents.

Action Step:

- List your current income sources. Are they active or passive?
- Identify at least one area where you can begin building an additional stream (e.g., side hustle, rental property, dividend investing).

STEP 2: ALIGN ASSETS WITH YOUR GOALS

An asset is anything that increases your net worth or provides positive cash flow. Many people confuse assets with liabilities. A car is not an asset if it loses value and costs you more than it brings in.

Examples of Wealth-Building Assets:

- Real estate with appreciating value or cash flow.
- Retirement and brokerage accounts.
- Profitable businesses.
- Intellectual property.
- Precious metals or collectibles (for long-term holding).

Avoid the trap of purchasing things that appear valuable but drain your resources. Focus on building assets that grow over time.

 The rich buy assets. The poor and middle class buy liabilities thinking they're assets."

ROBERT KIYOSAKI, *RICH DAD POOR DAD*

STEP 3: MASTER THE POWER OF CASH FLOW

You can earn $200,000 and still be broke if your expenses eat every dollar. Cash flow is the real difference-maker.

Cash Flow = Income − Expenses

Positive cash flow creates:

- Margin to invest.
- Space to give.
- Breathing room for peace of mind.

Action Step:

- Review your monthly cash flow. Is it positive, neutral, or negative?
- Identify opportunities to increase income, eliminate unnecessary expenses and automate savings/investments.

STEP 4: PROTECT WHAT YOU BUILD

A house with no roof is vulnerable. The same is true for your financial house.

Essentials:

- Insurance (life, disability, property).
- Estate documents (will, trust, power of attorney).
- Cybersecurity (password managers, identity protection).
- Legal business structure (LLC, S-Corp).

Stewardship includes not just creating wealth, but safeguarding it. You did not work hard to build, only to leave it all exposed. **Wealth without protection is fragile**.

> The prudent see danger and take refuge, but the simple keep going and pay the penalty."
>
> PROVERBS 27:12

STEP 5: DESIGN WITH FREEDOM IN MIND

Financial independence is not about extravagance—it is about options. True wealth means having the flexibility to choose how you live, work, rest, and give.

Ask yourself:

- What would you do if money were no longer a concern?
- What causes or projects would you support?
- How would your schedule, relationships, or career shift?

A good blueprint allows for both freedom of time and freedom of choice. That is the goal.

Dr. Olumide Emmanuel teaches:

> Financial freedom is not about having more

money; it's about being able to choose how you live."

A WEALTH BLUEPRINT IN PRACTICE: CASE STUDY

Name: Diana, 38

Profession: High school teacher

Income: $65,000 salary

Additional Income:

- $200/month from a rental property

Assets:

- $80,000 in a 403(b) retirement plan
- $25,000 in a Roth IRA
- $60,000 in home equity

Cash Flow:

- Surplus of $600 per month after all expenses

Plan:

- Invest $300/month into ETFs.
- Save $150/month toward a second rental property.
- Create a digital product to generate passive income.
- Establish a living trust for estate protection.

Diana is not wealthy by traditional standards, but she is on her way. Her wealth is being built with intention and clarity.

SCHOLAR'S LENS: SYSTEMS > EMOTION

From an academic perspective, one of the biggest predictors of wealth is **consistency**, not emotional decisions, windfalls, or risky bets.

Wealthy people don't make perfect decisions—they make repeatable, system-based ones:

- Automated investing and saving.
- Quarterly net worth tracking.
- Annual financial goal review.
- Regular rebalancing of portfolios.

Consistency wins over intensity. It is better to invest modestly every month for 20 years than to make sporadic, impulsive moves. If your system is sound, your results will follow.

REFLECTION QUESTIONS

1. What are your current income streams? Are they diversified?
2. What is one additional income stream you feel equipped to explore?
3. Are you building assets or accumulating liabilities?

4. How can you strengthen your systems for cash flow, investment, or protection?

KEY TAKEAWAYS

- Wealth is not just income—it is strategy, structure, and stewardship.
- Multiple income streams reduce risk and increase resilience.
- True wealth includes protection, purpose, and freedom.
- Your Wealth Blueprint should evolve as you grow—keep it living.

Next up: We will define what financial freedom really means—and how to move beyond numbers to a life of meaning, rest, and lasting purpose.

CHAPTER 8
DEFINING FINANCIAL FREEDOM

MOVING BEYOND NET WORTH TO DESIGN A LIFE THAT WORKS FOR YOU

The term "financial freedom" is often thrown around in personal finance circles, yet many individuals have never paused to define what it truly means for them. For some, it is the ability to retire early. For others, it is having the choice to work for passion rather than necessity, to travel freely, or to give generously without hesitation or guilt.

This chapter is about clarifying your personal definition of freedom. Financial freedom is not just about how much money you accumulate—it is about how intentionally you live. It is about creating space to breathe, to give, to rest, and to move through life with peace and purpose. True financial freedom aligns your resources with your vision.

WHAT FINANCIAL FREEDOM IS—AND WHAT IT IS NOT

Let us begin with what it is not:

- It is not merely being rich.
- It is not reaching a specific number in your investment account.
- It is not quitting your job just because you are tired of working.

And what it is:

- It is the power to choose how you live, work, and give.
- It is the absence of financial anxiety and the constant grind of survival mode.
- It is the alignment between your money and your mission.

Put simply: Financial freedom is about options, not opulence.

As Paul instructed in Galatians 5:13,

> 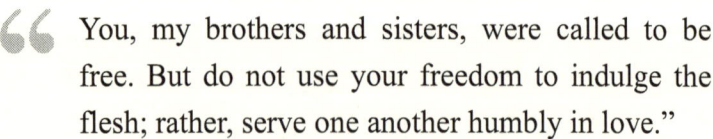 You, my brothers and sisters, were called to be free. But do not use your freedom to indulge the flesh; rather, serve one another humbly in love."

Freedom, even financial freedom, must be used purposefully.

THE FIVE LEVELS OF FINANCIAL FREEDOM

Freedom is not binary—it is progressive. Below are five stages that help clarify your current position and your next destination:

1. **Survival Freedom** Your basic needs are met. You are no longer living paycheck to paycheck.
2. **Stability Freedom** You have savings, no toxic debt, and a budget with margin.
3. **Flexibility Freedom** You can take time off, switch jobs, or pivot careers without crisis.
4. **Independence Freedom** Your investments and passive income cover your lifestyle needs.
5. **Legacy Freedom** You are funding causes, leaving wealth to the next generation, and making a lasting impact.

> Too many people spend money they have not earned, to buy things they do not want, to impress people they do not like."
>
> — WILL ROGERS

Ask yourself: What level describes your current life? What would it take to reach the next?

THE FOUR PILLARS OF TRUE FREEDOM

1. Clarity Know what "enough" looks like for you. Track your numbers. Get honest about your goals.

2. Consistency Build systems—not just routines. Automate savings and investments. Stick to your plan.

3. Margin Create space—financially and emotionally. Freedom cannot exist where there is pressure.

4. Purpose Let your values direct your goals. Money without a mission leads to burnout or emptiness.

Freedom is not just about escaping work—it is about doing meaningful work without fear or financial chains.

PURPOSE-DRIVEN WEALTH

True freedom is not just about what you get—it is about who you become.

The parable of the talents in Matthew 25 reminds us that God expects us to steward what we have been given. One servant was given five talents, another two, and another one. The first two multiplied their talents and were rewarded. The one who buried his talent out of fear was reprimanded.

Freedom is not hiding in safety—it is walking by faith. When you understand that **financial freedom is a tool, not a trophy**, you will begin to use money with boldness and clarity.

You can be debt-free and still feel bound. You can be wealthy and still feel hollow.

True freedom includes emotional, spiritual, and relational peace. You are not truly free if you are constantly anxious about money, if you are unable to give freely, or if you sacrifice your health and family to keep up appearances.

Purpose brings fulfillment. When your spending, giving, and investing align with your calling, you will experience the peace that money alone cannot provide.

I often remind my clients: "God is not trying to take something from you—He is trying to get something to you and through you."

HOW TO PURSUE YOUR FINANCIAL FREEDOM

- Define your ideal lifestyle.
- Set clear milestones.
- Eliminate financial clutter.
- Build automated income.
- Create a giving plan.
- Design your legacy.

YOUR FREEDOM NUMBER

Although freedom is not defined solely by numbers, it does require financial clarity.

Your Freedom Number is the amount of monthly income you need to live your ideal life without relying on active work.

Steps to calculate it:

1. Add up your realistic monthly living expenses (housing, food, transportation, giving, fun).
2. Multiply by 12 to get your annual amount.
3. Divide that number by a conservative withdrawal rate (4–5%) to estimate your target nest egg.

Example:

- Monthly lifestyle: $5,000
- Annual: $60,000
- Target investment return: 5%
- Required portfolio: $1.2 million

This is not a number to fear—it is a goal to plan for. You may not need it all at once, but knowing the target creates focus.

MINI FREEDOMS MATTER TOO

You do not need to wait until retirement to feel free. Celebrate the smaller milestones:

- Paying off your car.
- Taking a vacation without credit cards.
- Leaving a toxic work environment.

- Saying "yes" to an unpaid opportunity that aligns with your purpose.

These wins matter. They create momentum and build belief.

SCHOLAR'S INSIGHT: FREEDOM IS DYNAMIC

From a financial theory perspective, freedom is not a destination. It is a moving target based on your income, goals, and lifestyle.

What feels like freedom in your thirties may change by your fifties. That is why flexibility and reflection are crucial.

You must periodically revisit your goals, reset your systems, and realign your vision. Freedom evolves—your strategy should, too.

REFLECTION QUESTIONS

1. What does financial freedom mean to you—practically and emotionally?
2. Which level of freedom are you currently at?
3. What habits, beliefs, or barriers are holding you back from the next level?
4. Are your financial decisions leading you toward freedom—or away from it?

KEY TAKEAWAYS

- Financial freedom is personal—define it on your terms.
- There are progressive levels of freedom: survival, stability, flexibility, independence, and legacy.
- Freedom requires clarity, consistency, margin, and purpose.
- Celebrate small wins while building toward long-term independence.
- Real freedom includes emotional peace, not just financial security.

Next up: Now that you have begun building wealth and defining freedom, it is time to protect what you have worked so hard to create—with insurance, estate planning, and legacy-minded decisions that secure your future.

CHAPTER 9
PROTECT WHAT YOU BUILD

SAFEGUARDING YOUR WEALTH, FAMILY, AND FUTURE FROM THE UNEXPECTED

You have saved, budgeted, invested, and begun building real financial momentum. However, a single crisis—an accident, lawsuit, illness, or death—can undo years of progress. That is why protecting what you build is not optional. It is essential.

This chapter focuses on creating a safety net around your wealth, your family, and your future. You do not protect assets out of fear. You protect them out of wisdom, stewardship, and love for those who depend on you.

WHY PROTECTION MATTERS

You would not leave your front door wide open overnight. Likewise, you should not leave your financial future exposed.

Protection is not just about money—it is about peace of mind. A solid plan gives you confidence that your family will be cared for, your business will survive, and your legacy will endure.

Wealth without protection is like a roofless house—impressive from a distance but vulnerable to every storm.

THE PURPOSE OF PROTECTION

Most people avoid talking about protection—it feels morbid, complex, or unnecessary. But protection isn't about fear. It's about **responsibility**.

> True wealth isn't just what you accumulate—it's what you preserve and pass on."
>
> DR. BOLA "OBINNA" BOASMANBOON

You don't need to be wealthy to need protection. In fact, you need protection **precisely because** you're building wealth.

THE FOUR CORE AREAS OF PROTECTION

Insurance is not an investment—it's a shield. Its job is to absorb risk so you don't have to. Here's a breakdown of the must-haves:

1. Insurance—The Financial Shield

- **Health Insurance:** Covers unexpected medical costs—one of the leading causes of bankruptcy.

If you're employed, review your plan annually. If self-employed, explore options via healthcare.gov or faith-based health share plans (as a temporary bridge, not a long-term substitute).

- **Life Insurance:** Provides income replacement for dependents if you pass away. Term life is affordable and sufficient for most families. Permanent life may be useful for estate or tax planning.

Start with **term life**—10 to 12 times your annual income, especially if you have young children, a spouse, or debts.

- **Disability Insurance:** Replaces income if you are unable to work due to injury or illness.

Often overlooked, but absolutely essential—especially for single-income household.

- **Auto and Homeowners/Renters Insurance:** Covers damage, theft, liability, and natural disasters.
- **Umbrella Insurance:** Adds an extra layer of liability coverage once your net worth grows.

Tip: Buy coverage while you are young and healthy. It is cheaper and more accessible.

2. Estate Planning—Protecting Your Wishes and Your Family

No one likes to talk about wills and end-of-life matters. But ignoring them doesn't make them disappear. In fact, failing to plan can create confusion, conflict, and costly legal battles for your loved ones.

If you die without a will, the state decides what happens to your money, children, and property. So, make sure appropriate steps are taken right away. Estate planning is an act of clarity and care.

Here's what you need, regardless of age, income, or net worth:

- **Will**: Outlines who receives your assets and who will become guardian of your children.
- **Durable Power of Attorney**: Appoints someone to manage your financial affairs if you are incapacitated.
- **Healthcare Proxy / Medical Power of Attorney**: Names someone to make medical decisions on your behalf.
- **Living Will (Advance Healthcare Directive):** States your preferences regarding life-sustaining treatment, if you are unable to communicate.
- **Revocable Living Trust**: Allows your estate to bypass probate, saving time and court costs. It also provides privacy, continuity, and control – especially helpful if

you own property in multiple states or have minor beneficiaries.

Benefits of a Living Trust:

- **Avoids probate**—no need for your estate to be tied up in court.
- **Ensures privacy**—unlike wills, trusts are not public record.
- **Manages assets across state lines**—ideal if you own property in multiple states.
- **Allows for ongoing control**—you can update, amend, or revoke the trust during your lifetime.
- **Protects dependents**—set rules for how and when heirs receive money (especially minor children or financially immature beneficiaries).

Think of a **TRUST** like a **vault**. You place your valuable assets inside, appoint someone to manage it (a trustee), and leave instructions on when and how to distribute the contents.

🛠 **Action Step: Create Your Must-Have Documents**

Use affordable, attorney-approved services like:

- **Suze Orman's Will & Trust Kit**
- **Trust & Will**
- **LegalZoom** for more customized guidance

Tip: Review these documents every 3 to 5 years or after major life changes (marriage, divorce, children, relocation), and share a copy with a trusted family member or executor and store securely (physically and digitally).

> These documents are not for when you die – they are for while you are alive but can't speak for yourself."
>
> SUZE ORMAN

3. Cyber and Identity Protection—Your Digital Defense

We now live in a digital-first world, and your financial life now lives online. Protecting your digital footprint is part of your wealth strategy.

Steps to Protect:

- Use a password manager with strong, unique passwords.
- Enable two-factor authentication on financial and email accounts.
- Shred financial documents before discarding.
- Monitor your credit regularly through free sites or paid services.
- Freeze your credit if you are not applying for new loans.
- Consider identity theft protection plans if your risk is high.

4. Legal Protection—Covering the Details

As you grow in business and wealth, legal protection becomes more important.

- LLC or Corporation: Use these structures to separate your personal and business finances.
- Contracts: Always use written agreements, even with friends or family.
- Professional Help: When in doubt, consult with an attorney or estate planner. The cost of advice is often less than the cost of mistakes.

A LEGACY THAT ENDURES

Protection is not about living in fear - Proverbs 13:22 teaches, "A good man leaves an inheritance to his children's children." That inheritance is not only financial—it is also clarity, peace of mind, and protection from unnecessary chaos.

Planning for death, illness, or disaster may feel uncomfortable, but it is a form of love in action. It ensures that your loved ones will not be left sorting through confusion in the midst of grief.

You are not building wealth to show off. You are building it to serve, and to serve others best is a plan that stands, even when you are no longer here.

SCHOLAR'S LENS: RISK MANAGEMENT IN PRACTICE

From a financial planning perspective, protection is risk mitigation. It will not prevent all losses, but it reduces your exposure to catastrophic ones.

The most successful individuals and institutions use insurance, legal entities, and estate tools not as luxury extras—but as strategic necessities. It is not about pessimism. It is about preparation.

REFLECTION QUESTIONS

1. Do you have adequate life, health, and property insurance? When did you last review it?
2. Have you prepared a will or any other estate documents? If not, what is holding you back?
3. How secure is your digital life? What steps can you take this month to improve it?
4. Are you operating with proper legal protections in your business or investments?

KEY TAKEAWAYS

- Protection is not fear—it is wisdom in action.
- Insurance, estate planning, and digital security are essential components of financial health.

- Legal and digital vulnerabilities can undo years of progress if left unchecked.
- Stewardship includes safeguarding not just what you earn but also what you leave behind.

Next up: In the final chapter, we will bring everything together – connecting your money, mission, and purpose so that your financial life reflects not only success but also significance.

CHAPTER 10
WEALTH, FAITH & PURPOSE

ALIGNING YOUR MONEY WITH MEANING THAT LASTS

You have learned how to manage money wisely, build wealth intentionally, and protect what you create. However, one final question remains that brings everything into focus: What is it all for?

Financial freedom without purpose is hollow. Wealth without wisdom can become dangerous. Financial success that does not reflect your values is simply noise—not legacy. True success with money must reflect who you are, what you believe, and what you are called to do.

This chapter is about integration—connecting your money to your mission and ensuring that your financial life reflects your highest values. Money is a tool, not a purpose. Your career may generate income. Your investments may produce returns.

However, only purpose brings fulfillment.

PURPOSE OVER PROFIT

Purpose provides direction for wealth. It helps you determine:

- What to pursue.
- What to walk away from.
- What to give, build, and protect.

When your financial life aligns with your life's calling, you are no longer driven by pressure—you are guided by purpose. You stop chasing 'more' for the sake of ego or comparison and start building 'meaning' for the sake of legacy and impact.

WHAT PURPOSE-DRIVEN WEALTH LOOKS LIKE

- You choose work that reflects your values—not just your paycheck.
- You spend in ways that express your priorities—not just your emotions.
- You give generously without fear of lack
- You invest in people, projects, and causes that bring positive change—your church, your community, your children.
- You build something that will outlive you—a business, a foundation, a movement.

Purpose transforms money from a survival mechanism into a tool for service. Purpose is the compass, and wealth is the vehicle. Without a compass, the vehicle goes in circles.

FAITH AND FINANCES: A HIGHER CALLING

Across faith traditions, wealth is seen not as a reward but as a responsibility. You are not the ultimate owner of what you possess. You are a steward.

This mindset changes everything:

- You stop asking, "What can I afford?" and begin asking, "What am I called to do?"
- You stop measuring wealth by what you consume and begin measuring it by what you contribute.
- You stop fearing lack and begin trusting that you have been entrusted with something sacred.

As stated in 1 Corinthians 4:2 (KJV),

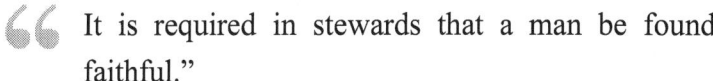 It is required in stewards that a man be found faithful."

Stewardship means managing what is placed in your hands with wisdom, integrity, and impact.

THE THREEFOLD PURPOSE OF WEALTH

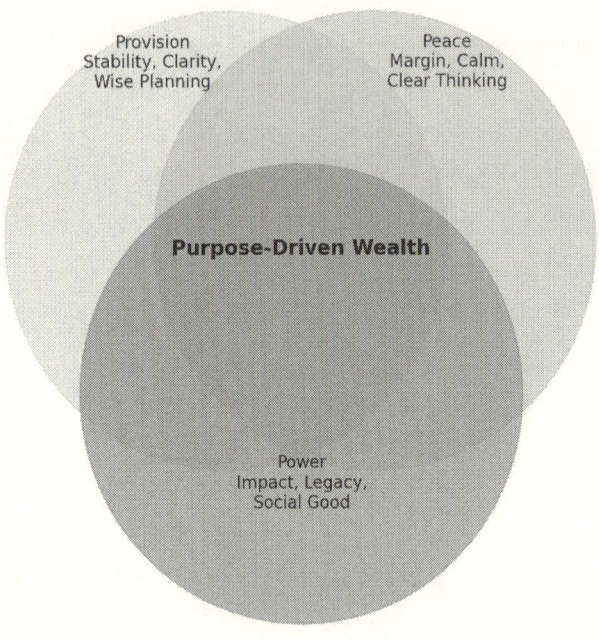

This diagram illustrates how provision, peace, and power work together to give your wealth direction and depth.

1. **Provision**

Take care of yourself and your household. Build systems that promote financial clarity, savings, and resilience. Budgeting and planning help keep your house in order.

2. **Peace**

Create margin that allows you to think clearly, avoid anxiety-driven decisions, and rest. Money does not purchase peace, but it can fund the conditions where peace is possible.

3. **Power**

Use your resources to influence positive change. Support important causes, amplify marginalized voices, and help break cycles of poverty or injustice. Power, when aligned with purpose, becomes legacy.

DESIGNING A GIVING STRATEGY

Generosity does not require excess—it requires intention. You do not need to be wealthy to give. You only need to be willing. Planned giving is just as impactful as planned investing. Make generosity a consistent part of your monthly financial plan.

Ways to give include:

- Financial gifts
- Volunteering time or expertise
- Sponsoring students, ministries, or mission work
- Offering anonymous support to individuals in need
- Mentoring or developing future leaders

Giving multiplies wealth in ways that cannot be measured on a spreadsheet. It also ensures that your heart remains aligned with your values.

LEGACY: WHAT WILL OUTLIVE YOU?

Real wealth is not measured by what you spend. It is measured by what continues after you are gone. **Legacy is not about possessions—it is about principles.**

Ask yourself:

- What values will I pass down to my children or community?
- What systems am I putting in place to preserve what I have built?
- What story will be told about how I lived and what I gave?

Your legacy might include:

- A trust or estate that blesses future generations
- A scholarship fund in your name
- Financial wisdom passed down through lived example
- A business or nonprofit that continues to impact lives
- A reputation for stewardship, integrity, and faith

Legacy is not reserved for the ultra-wealthy. It is built by anyone who lives with intention and finishes with purpose.

SCHOLAR'S LENS: BEYOND ROI TO ROE—RETURN ON ETERNITY

As someone trained in finance at the highest levels, I understand the value of ROI—Return on Investment. However, there is a higher metric we must also evaluate: Return on Eternity (ROE).

ROE reflects the impact your money has beyond your lifetime—the lives changed, the communities served, the vision you helped bring to life. Whether through philanthropy, ethical investing, sustainable enterprise, or spiritual giving, your money can do more than grow—it can give life.

This is where wealth becomes meaningful. And this is where purpose becomes permanent.

REFLECTION QUESTIONS

1. What does wealth mean to you—beyond income or assets?
2. Who are you called to support, serve, or uplift with your financial resources?
3. What is one step you can take to align your finances with your values?
4. What legacy would make you most proud, even if you never witness its full impact?

KEY TAKEAWAYS

- Money is a tool—not the ultimate goal. Purpose gives it direction.
- Financial success must be matched with stewardship and integrity.
- Wealth includes provision, peace, and power used for good.
- Generosity and legacy begin with daily decisions.
- Your life has value. Your money can reflect that—now and for generations to come.

CHAPTER 11
FROM FINANCIAL STABILITY TO GENERATIONAL IMPACT

 A good person leaves an inheritance for their children's children."

PROVERBS 13:22

Financial stability is an achievement. Generational impact is a responsibility.

Most people begin their financial journey focused on survival—paying bills, managing debt, and meeting daily obligations. As progress is made, attention shifts to comfort, flexibility, and personal freedom. These milestones are significant and deserve recognition. However, when financial growth ends with personal comfort, its influence is limited to a single lifetime.

Scripture consistently points beyond personal sufficiency toward continuity and foresight. Financial maturity is not only about provision for today but preparation for tomorrow. This chapter explores the shift from individual financial stability to intentional generational influence.

RETHINKING WEALTH: BEYOND INCOME AND NET WORTH

> The plans of the diligent lead surely to abundance."
>
> PROVERBS 21:5

Traditional measures of financial success, income levels and net worth, provide useful snapshots but fail to capture long-term durability. Income can be disrupted. Net worth can fluctuate. Even significant assets can erode if they are not supported by structure, discipline, and understanding.

Wealth, in its truest form, is defined by sustainability. It is the ability to absorb financial shocks, adapt to changing circumstances, and continue functioning without constant intervention. Wealth is not merely what exists today; it is what continues tomorrow.

Short-term financial thinking emphasizes consumption and visible rewards. Long-term thinking emphasizes structure, preservation, and transferability. Scripture reinforces this distinction by consistently elevating planning, diligence, and foresight over impulsive gain.

Rethinking wealth requires a shift from a transactional mindset to a systems mindset. Rather than asking, "How much do I earn?" the more meaningful question becomes, "What continues to work even when I am no longer actively involved?"

THE DIFFERENCE BETWEEN INHERITANCE AND LEGACY

Inheritance is the transfer of assets. Legacy is the transfer of understanding.

Many families pass down money, property, or businesses without passing down the wisdom required to manage them. The result is often confusion, conflict, or rapid depletion. Wealth without preparation becomes a burden rather than a blessing.

Legacy extends beyond financial resources. It includes decision-making frameworks, values around stewardship, and systems that guide behavior over time. Scripture repeatedly connects provision with wisdom, emphasizing that resources alone do not guarantee stability.

Legacy planning requires intentionality. It involves explaining not only what is being passed down but why. This clarity transforms inheritance into stewardship and prepares future generations to manage both opportunity and responsibility.

FINANCIAL LITERACY AS A MULTIGENERATIONAL RESPONSIBILITY

 Train up a child in the way he should go, and when he is old, he will not depart from it."

PROVERBS 22:6

Financial literacy is cultivated, not inherited. Yet in many households, money remains a taboo subject discussed only during moments of stress. This silence creates gaps in understanding that often surface during pivotal life decisions.

Effective financial education evolves across life stages. Children learn through observation and modeling. Teenagers learn through responsibility and practice. Young adults require structure and guidance. Mature adults and heirs require strategy, accountability, and stewardship.

Normalizing financial dialogue builds confidence rather than dependency. It reduces fear, secrecy, and misunderstanding. When families intentionally teach financial principles, wealth becomes resilient rather than fragile.

ASSETS THAT OUTLIVE YOU: BUILDING DURABLE WEALTH SYSTEMS

 Suppose one of you wants to build a tower. Will he not first sit down and estimate the cost?

LUKE 14:28

Generational impact is built on assets designed to endure beyond individual involvement. Scripture consistently affirms planning before building and structure before expansion.

Durable wealth systems generate income rather than consume it. They are documented, transferable, and aligned with long-term goals. Examples include income-producing real estate, businesses with transferable operations, diversified investment portfolios, and properly structured trusts.

These systems are designed to function with or without daily oversight. While they require discipline and delayed gratification during the building phase, they offer continuity and stability across generations.

PURPOSE-DRIVEN WEALTH AND STRATEGIC GIVING

 Each of you should give what you have decided in your heart to give, not reluctantly or under compulsion."

2 CORINTHIANS 9:7

Purpose gives wealth direction. Without purpose, financial success can feel disconnected from meaning. Purpose-driven wealth aligns financial decisions with values, allowing generosity without financial instability.

Strategic giving involves intention rather than impulse. It includes defined causes, planned contributions, and long-term sustainability. Scripture affirms generosity that flows from wisdom and clarity, reinforcing stewardship rather than undermining it.

When generosity is structured, it becomes a teaching tool for future generations—demonstrating responsibility, compassion, and discipline.

CREATING A PERSONAL LEGACY BLUEPRINT

 Plans succeed with counsel."

PROVERBS 20:18

A legacy does not form by chance. It is the result of clarity, communication, and documentation. A personal legacy blueprint provides guidance when personal explanation is no longer possible.

Key components include estate and succession planning documents, clear beneficiary designations, written financial values or family mission statements, and regular family discussions.

Scripture consistently emphasizes counsel, preparation, and wisdom in planning.

Legacy planning is not about control; it is about clarity. It protects relationships as much as it protects resources and ensures that what has been built continues to serve its intended purpose.

REFLECTION QUESTIONS

1. How does your understanding of wealth extend beyond income and net worth?
2. What systems are you intentionally building to support long-term continuity?
3. How comfortable are you with discussing financial stewardship across generations?
4. What values do you want your financial legacy to reflect?

KEY TAKEAWAYS

 The wise store up choice food and olive oil."

PROVERBS 21:20

Financial stability provides comfort. Generational impact provides continuity.

The true measure of wealth is not how much is accumulated, but how well it endures. When wealth is structured with wisdom, education, and purpose, it becomes more than a personal achievement—it becomes a lasting contribution.

As this chapter brings the discussion from financial stability to generational impact, it also brings this book to its natural point of reflection. The principles explored throughout *Financially Grounded* were never intended to exist in isolation, but to work together—guiding decisions, shaping habits, and building systems that endure.

The conclusion that follows is not an ending, but an invitation: to apply what has been learned, to move forward with clarity and confidence, and to commit to a financial life that is intentional, disciplined, and purpose-driven.

LIVING FINANCIALLY GROUNDED

Financial grounding is not achieved through a single decision or a moment of motivation. It is the result of consistent, informed choices made over time. It is built through awareness, structure, and accountability.

Throughout this book, you have been introduced to foundational principles designed to help you eliminate debt, build wealth, and define financial freedom on your own terms. These principles are practical, but they are also personal. They require honesty, patience, and commitment.

Being financially grounded means understanding not only how money works, but how it works for you. It means aligning financial decisions with values, goals, and long-term vision rather than short-term pressure or comparison. It means recognizing that wealth is not simply accumulated, but managed, protected, and transferred with intention.

This journey does not require perfection. It requires progress. There will be seasons of acceleration and seasons of recalibration. What matters is the willingness to remain engaged, informed, and intentional.

As you move forward, remember that your financial life has influence beyond your personal circumstances. The habits you build, the systems you design, and the decisions you make today shape the opportunities available tomorrow.

This is what it means to live financially grounded.

FINAL WORDS: YOUR JOURNEY STARTS NOW

This book was never about perfection. It was always about progress. You may not have everything figured out yet. That is perfectly acceptable. What matters most is that you are no longer drifting—you are now grounded.

You have the tools. You have the knowledge. You have the clarity. The next step belongs to you.

Start where you are. Use what you have. And never forget this truth:

> FINANCIAL FREEDOM IS NOT A FANTASY.
> IT IS A DECISION.

And you are fully capable of making that decision—starting today.

Writing *Financially Grounded* has been both a professional and personal endeavor. Over the years, I have observed that financial challenges are rarely rooted in a lack of income alone, but in a lack of structure, clarity, and intentionality. This book was written to help bridge that gap.

My hope is that the principles shared here serve not only as information, but as guidance—tools you can return to as your financial life evolves. Financial grounding is not about perfection or comparison. It is about progress, discipline, and purpose.

Wherever you are on your journey, remember that sustainable financial growth is built one decision at a time. When money is managed with wisdom and intention, it becomes a resource that supports stability, freedom, and long-term impact.

Thank you for allowing this book to be part of your journey.

Dr. Bola Obinna Boasmanboon

NEXT STEPS
CONTINUING YOUR FINANCIALLY JOURNEY

The principles in *Financially Grounded* are designed to be applied, revisited, and refined over time. Financial growth is not a one-time event, but an ongoing process that evolves with each season of life.

As you move forward, consider documenting your progress, revisiting your financial goals regularly, and continuing your education. Tools such as companion workbooks, coaching programs, and structured financial reviews can provide accountability and clarity as your circumstances change.

Most importantly, remain intentional. Financial grounding is sustained through awareness, discipline, and consistent action.

RESOURCES & CONTINUED SUPPORT

Financial literacy is a lifelong pursuit, and continued growth is strengthened through learning, accountability, and community. Readers who wish to deepen their understanding and apply the principles in this book more intentionally are encouraged to seek ongoing education and professional guidance through #iamfinanciallygrounded on social media platforms.

Financial coaching provides a structured environment to assess goals, address challenges, and design personalized strategies for debt elimination, wealth building, and long-term financial planning. Coaching offers clarity, accountability, and support as financial priorities evolve through different seasons of life.

You are also invited to engage in the broader *Financially Grounded* community through social media. Shared insights, reflections, and practical guidance are provided to support continued learning and encouragement.

Follow and join the conversation using
#iamfinanciallygrounded

Made in the USA
Middletown, DE
24 January 2026